ATTACK OF
THE KILLER
FROGS

First published 2012 by A & C Black,
an imprint of Bloomsbury Publishing Plc
50 Bedford Square, London WC1B 3DP

www.acblack.com
www.bloomsbury.com

ISBN 978-1-4081-5268-3

This book is produced using paper that is made from wood
grown in managed, sustainable forests. It is natural, renewable
and recyclable. The logging and manufacturing processes conform
to the environmental regulations of the country of origin.

Printed by CPI Group (UK), Croydon, CR0 4YY

1 3 5 7 9 8 6 4 2

recommended by

Catch Up®

www.catchup.org

Catch Up is a not-for-profit charity
which aims to address the problem of
underachievement that has its roots in
literacy and numeracy difficulties.

ATTACK of THE KILLER FROGS

PETER CLOVER

A & C Black • London

For Hus. 'Per sempre.'

Contents

Chapter One   On Holiday   7

Chapter Two   The Trap   15

Chapter Three   Trapped!   25

Chapter Four   Night Noises   32

Chapter Five   The Frogs are Coming...   40

Chapter Six   Attack!   47

Chapter Seven   Old One-Eye   56

Chapter One

On Holiday

Lily sat by the pond at the end of Rose Cottage's garden.

The fields around her belonged to a company called Blue Harvest. Blue Harvest made chemicals.

Blue Harvest owned all the land around there, except for Rose Cottage.

Rose Cottage belonged to Lily's family. They spent every summer holiday there. Dad did not want to sell the cottage to Blue Harvest.

Mum said, "Blue Harvest do odd things. I don't trust them."

Lily and Missy, her big ginger cat, were sitting on a flat stone at the edge of the pond. Lily wanted to listen to the frogs.

As the sun dipped behind the trees, Lily heard the first croak.

But it wasn't a normal frog sound. It was more of a growl. And it was close.

Missy flattened her ears and hissed.

Lily had listened to frogs lots of times. That croak was wrong.

The frog growled again. It sounded angry.

Missy turned and fled back to the cottage.

Slowly, the reeds bent, snapping as something heavy pushed through.

Lily's mouth dropped open.

The frog was huge. Its skin was covered in green slime. It stared at Lily with bulging, yellow eyes.

"That can't be a frog," thought Lily. "It's bigger than my cat!"

Lily stared at the frog. The frog stared back. Its eyes looked cold and evil.

The frog's mouth opened, showing razor sharp teeth.

Lily tried to scream, but nothing came out.

She jumped to her feet and ran back to the cottage.

Lily ran into the kitchen and slammed the back door.

"Frogs!" That was all Lily could say as she threw herself into Mum's arms, sobbing. "Frogs!"

Chapter Two

The Trap

The next morning at breakfast, Lily hardly said a word.

"You're very quiet," said Mum. "Are you still thinking about that silly frog?"

"Giant frogs!" Dad laughed.

Lily didn't think it was funny. "Why don't they believe me?" she thought.

"How big was it, again?" teased Dad.

"I didn't make it up," said Lily.

Her parents smiled at each other.

"I'll catch that giant frog and then they'll believe me," thought Lily.

Lily found an old suitcase in the shed.

She took it to the big stone by the pond. She lifted the lid.

The open suitcase looked like a mouth, waiting to swallow a frog.

Lily took some string and tied one end to a short stick. She used the stick to prop open the lid of the suitcase.

She pulled the string to test her trap. The stick popped out and the lid of the case slammed shut.

"Cool!" cried Lily. "But how do I make the frog go in the case?"

She thought for a moment.

"I've got it! Jaffa cakes. Everyone loves Jaffa cakes."

That evening, Lily took three Jaffa cakes and went outside.

Missy stayed behind. She hadn't left the cottage all day.

Lily ate one Jaffa cake and tossed the other two into the open suitcase. Then she set the trap, hid behind a bush, and waited.

From her hiding place, Lily could see the Blue Harvest lab. The fields around Blue Harvest were very bright green. They seemed too green to be real.

Everything was too quiet. No birds sang. The only noise she could hear was the low rumble of a farm machine on the Blue Harvest fields.

The machine came closer. Lily heard a soft hissing.

It sounded like something being sprayed through a high pressure hose.

A strong chemical smell filled the air. It stung Lily's eyes.

She put a hand over her mouth.

Lily didn't want to breathe the spray. She thought it might make her sick.

Lily didn't notice the reeds on the far side of the pond start to move...

Chapter Three

Trapped!

A huge, flat head forced its way through the reeds. Yellow eyes fixed Lily with an evil glare. Slimy snot bubbled as the frog sniffed the air.

The giant frog peered over the side of the suitcase.

Then it jumped inside – and knocked the stick that held the trap open.

Lily jumped up as the suitcase slammed shut. She put a big rock on top of the case to stop the frog from getting out.

Then she raced back to the cottage.

"Come and look, quick. I've caught the mutant frog!" Lily cried. She pulled Mum through the door. Dad followed with a big grin on his face.

"There," said Lily when they reached the pond. She pointed to the case. "I've trapped it."

Dad moved the rock and lifted the lid. "Argh!"

Lily jumped with fright. But Mum and Dad were laughing. Dad held up the empty case.

"If you are going to hunt giant killer frogs," said Dad, "make sure there are no holes in your traps."

He showed her a big hole in the suitcase.

"That wasn't there before," Lily said. "The frog chewed its way out!"

The worst bit was that Lily's parents thought it was all a joke.

Hidden from sight, hungry yellow eyes gazed at Lily's pink toes. Two giant frogs licked their lips.

Chapter Four

Night Noises

At tea-time, Dad put his arm around Lily.

"Sorry I laughed at you," he said.

"Maybe it was a ferret you trapped. Or a
rat."

"It was a frog!" Lily yelled. She stormed out of the room.

Rose Cottage only had one bedroom. Lily slept downstairs on a sofa bed. Normally, she thought it was cool. But tonight she was scared.

Lily pulled a chair across the cat flap in the back door.

Then she fell asleep – until an awful scream woke her.

Lily sat bolt upright.

The chair in front of the door had fallen over. The cat flap was hanging open. Missy was gone.

"What the heck was that?" Dad clomped down the stairs.

Clumps of Missy's fur were stuck to the cat flap frame. There was blood. And a slimy wet frog footprint – *inside* the house.

"A fox, maybe," said Dad. "Missy must have chased it off." He grabbed a torch and headed outside.

Lily saw another slimy frog footprint. Then another. And another.

She followed the prints to her sofa bed and found a big green puddle that smelled a bit like cat's pee.

"Can't find Missy anywhere," Dad said.

"I hope she's OK," said Lily. "There was blood on the cat flap!"

"Only a few drops," said Dad.

"What about those webbed footprints?" said Lily. "And that big green puddle?"

"What footprints?" asked Dad.

Lily pointed, but the frog prints had already dried up.

Mum looked at the puddle.

"Well, Missy did that," she said, and went to fetch a mop.

"I think it's the frogs," Lily said.

"I'm getting fed up with this frog nonsense." Dad sounded cross.

"Come on," said Mum. "All back to bed. Everything will seem better in the morning."

To Lily, morning seemed a long way off.
"Can I sleep upstairs with you?"

"No. I'm going to put my earplugs in,"
Mum said. "I've had enough of screaming.
I want a good night's sleep."

"Me too," said Dad. "Goodnight, Lily."

Chapter Five

The Frogs are Coming...

"I can't sleep down here with those horrid frogs around," said Lily.

She pulled on her jeans, then carried her pillows and duvet upstairs to the small landing.

Then she thought, "I must block the cat flap."

Lily dragged a log basket across the hole. She pulled the wooden handle off the mop-head, and took it upstairs.

After less than an hour, she was fast asleep.

She had left a lamp on downstairs. Pale light shone across the floor and up the stairs to the landing.

Behind the closed door, Mum and Dad
slept. Rose Cottage was silent.

Then it started.

Something very strong pushed the log
basket clear of the cat flap.

Lily woke as something soft yet heavy hit the floor with a 'flump'. Then another. And another.

She peered down the stairs.

Her jaw dropped open.

Five giant frogs were squatting by the back door. Ten yellow eyes glinted in the gloom.

Lily kept very still. Her heart pounded. She gripped the wooden mop handle like a spear.

"I should wake Mum and Dad!" she thought. But Lily didn't want to bang on the door in case the frogs heard her.

Besides, her parents used good earplugs. Nothing would wake them.

The cat flap rattled. A huge head slowly pushed through.

The biggest frog of them all forced its way inside.

Chapter Six

Attack!

This frog looked older than the others. It had one blind eye, like a cold, white marble.

Lily ducked out of sight. But her shadow danced across the wall. All six frogs saw it.

The frogs began to move.

The first one reached the bottom of the stairs. It climbed very fast.

Lily felt dizzy with fear. "They're going to eat me!"

She banged on the bedroom door.

"Mum! Dad! Help! Help me! The frogs are coming!"

The first frog reached the landing. The second was close behind.

Lily raised the wooden mop handle, and hit the frog as hard as she could.

The frog stumbled back and fell onto the one behind. They both tumbled down the stairs.

When the frogs hit the floor, they burst, melting into a gloopy, green puddle.

Three more frogs began to climb the stairs.

Lily banged on the door like crazy, but Mum and Dad were fast asleep.

The next frog to reach the top took Lily by surprise.

It leapt, knocking her back against the door. Its claws dug into her T-shirt. Lily felt its hot, foul breath on her face.

The second frog jumped. It landed on the back of the first frog.

There was a sound like a water balloon bursting, and Lily found herself covered in stinking green slime.

The second frog fell to the floor. It burst with a dull 'bloop' when it hit the ground.

The third frog snarled. Lily shoved the mop handle at it. The frog bit the end of the stick. Snap! The end came away, leaving a sharp point.

The frog tried to bite her leg. Its sharp teeth ripped a hole in her jeans.

Lily jabbed at the frog with the mop stick. The frog burst! Green gunk hit the walls.

Lily kicked at the door. "Mum! Dad!" She rattled the handle. "Wake up!"

Then she heard a low growl. Slowly, Lily turned around.

Old One-eye was on the landing. He was even bigger than Lily had thought – like a green space-hopper with legs.

Lily's mouth went dry. She leaned back against the door, too tired to move.

Chapter Seven

Old One-Eye

The big frog grinned with a mouthful of fangs. Green, gloopy spit dribbled onto the floor.

Lily was so scared she almost fell down.

Old One-eye lumbered towards her.

"Mum... Dad..." she whispered.

Then the door opened behind her and Lily fell into Dad's arms.

"What the – " Dad began.

The giant frog jumped at him. Dad pushed Lily aside just in time. The monster landed on his chest. Dad fell to the floor.

Mum screamed as Dad struggled with the huge frog.

Razor sharp teeth gnashed, inches from his face. The frog clawed at Dad, shredding his pyjamas.

Lily stabbed at the frog with her spear.

But this frog was much tougher than the others.

Dad kicked the frog away. Lily ran to his side.

Old One-Eye took a flying leap at him.

Lily held her stick out in front of her.
The frog landed right on its point. It fell
back, kicking.

Mum, Dad and Lily watched as the
monster frog slowly melted down into a
gloopy, stinking puddle.

Dad called the police. But it was hours before they came. And all the slimy puddles had dried up.

They told their story. They thought that Blue Harvest's strange chemicals had turned the frogs into monsters.

"But there's nothing here," said the policeman. "There's no proof!"

Suddenly, there was a loud, "Meow!"

It was Missy. She was dragging something huge and slimy through the cat flap.

'Missy!" said Lily. "You're OK!"

Lily scooped up the ginger cat. Then she stared down, with the others, at the giant tadpole that gasped and squirmed on the floor.